MW00881634

©2024 by Andrew Mochrie
CYMT Press is an imprint of the Center for Youth Ministry Training, 309 Franklin
Road, Brentwood, Tennessee 37027

ISBN 9798325927584

New Revised Standard Version, New International Version Bible translation,
The Message and English Standard Version are used.

The website addresses listed in the book were current at the time of
publication. Please contact the Center for Youth Ministry Training via email
(info@cymt.org) to report URLs that are no longer operational and replacement
URLs if available.
Editorial Direction by Andrew Mochrie
Art Design by Judy Coursey
Proofreading by Stephen Ingram
Contributions by Tyler Hendon
Contributions by Kelsey Bryant
Contributions by Aaron Kick
Contributions by Jenna Schmidt
Contributions by Julia Elzinga
Contributions by Andrew Mochrie
Printed in the United States.

Hello
FRIENDS

We're so excited to learn, worship, and serve with you!

We hope that your eyes will be open and that your hearts and minds will be ready to see and experience God at work while you're here.

You might be wondering...what's the deal with this journal? We're glad you asked! The pages of this journal are filled with prompts, questions, and other activities to help you reflect, think, wonder, pray, and interact with your friends over the course of your time at CSM.

Where will you see God?
How will you experience the Holy Spirit at work?
What might transformation look like for you?

This journal is a tool to help you capture and articulate the mountaintop moments that make experiences like CSM so meaningful. So, keep it with you. Use it to connect deeper with God—with the people you serve and those who serve alongside you.

We're praying that you experience the love and acceptance of God in a new, life-changing way.

THIS JOURNAL BELONGS TO: _____

KANSAS CITY

HOUSING SITE: MOUNT OLIVE MISSIONARY BAPTIST
CHURCH (MT. OLIVE) KANSAS CITY, MISSOURI

*KCC exists to develop servant leaders who know God,
have a passion for holiness of heart, and are inspired and
prepared for a lifetime of learning and Kingdom service.*

Kansas City Bible College, as it was called at the beginning, started in 1938 in the Church of God (Holiness) at 29th and Askew in Kansas City, Mo. The founding president, Rev. A.C. Watkins, had long carried a desire to start a Bible college in the Kansas City area, and his church basement was the logical place to start. He rented nearby homes for dormitory space, and students came from across the Midwest and as far as Oregon to enroll in the new college and high school.

Since then the college has grown significantly but has remained focused on preparing students with the educational, social, and spiritual tools needed to be effective in the places that God led them.

Overland Park is a suburb of Kansas City but is included in the KC metropolitan area. It is the second largest city in Kansas (Wichita being #1) and surpassing Kansas City, KS because it is divided between 2 states. It was voted the "best city to raise a family" in 2018.

NEIGHBORHOODS

- Brookside
- Country Club Plaza
- Crossroads
- Crown Center District
- Downtown
- East Bottoms
- Jazz District (18th & Vine)
- Kansas City, KS (KCK)
- North KC
- River Market
- West Bottoms
- Westport
- Westside

FUN FACTS:

1. Kansas City has more barbeque restaurants per capita than any other US city.
2. Kansas City has over 300 fountains, nicknamed The City of Fountains.
3. Swope Park, at 1,805 acres, is more than twice the size of Central Park in New York City.
4. Walt Disney opened his first animation studio, Laugh-O-Gram Studios, in Kansas City. Mickey Mouse was potentially inspired by a real-life mouse in the building.
5. Hallmark, the largest greeting card maker in the world, was founded in KC in 1910 when J.C. Hall began selling postcards out of two shoeboxes at the local YMCA.

NASHVILLE

McKendree Church was started in 1787 by Rev. Benjamin Ogden.
To put this in a historical perspective, it was the same year our
forefathers wrote the Constitution. The first building was constructed
in 1833. It was named in honor of Bishop William McKendree, who
preached and dedicated the church building on November 23, 1834. It
was the largest Methodist church in the United States at the time. It was
converted into a hospital during the American Civil War of 1861-1865. The
funeral of James Polk, who served as the 11th President of the
United States, was conducted by Rev. McFerrin in this church.

McKendree has had four buildings. The first, completed in 1833, was heavily
damaged during the Civil War. The congregation decided in 1876 to take it
down and build a larger, more ornate church building. That second was
completed and dedicated in January 1879. Unfortunately, after the close
of the evening service on Sunday, October 26, the same year, the building
caught fire and was destroyed. The third was completed in 1882. It lasted
until July 4, 1905. On a hot day, the windows were open, and fireworks
accidentally came through, and again, the church was destroyed by fire. Our
present sanctuary was completed in 1910. The stained glass windows are
original to 1910. They are scenes from the life of Christ by various European
painters. The work was done by the Von Gerichten Art Glass Company of
Columbus, Ohio, shipped here by railroad, and installed as the church
building was erected.

NEIGHBORHOODS

- **Germantown** Known as Nashville's first suburb, Germantown is now considered urban living. As Nashville's first planned neighborhood, these 18 square blocks were the center of the local German community, thus, "Germantown."

- **Edgehill** Edgehill was the home of THREE different forts during the Civil War. However, it didn't expand much until the early 1900s. It is also home to the famed Music Row.

- **Donelson** James Robertson and John Donelson are the two men credited with settling Nashville. This part of Nashville takes its name from John Donelson. He was also the father-in-law of Andrew Jackson, the seventh president of the United States.

- **Eastwood** You can find Eastwood in East Nashville (shocker), and the first house in the neighborhood was built in 1849.

- **Sylvan Park** The area now known as Sylvan Park was once a popular place to escape city life in the late 1800s. The word "sylvan" means pleasantly rural and wooded, and this area was sought after for picnic escapes from city life. By the early 1900s, many of the area's homes had been built by Sylvan Park Land Company, and the area was now an official suburb of Nashville. One of the company's owners, James A. Bowling, named his neighborhood home "Sylvan Park," and the area has been known as that ever since.

FUN FACTS:

1. Nashville's Centennial Park is home to the only replica of the Greek Parthenon. A sculpture of Athena Parthenos inside the Parthenon is the tallest indoor sculpture in the western hemisphere at 42 feet high.

2. The tallest skyscraper in Tennessee, the 33-story AT&T Building is known around the world as the "Batman Building" because its facade resembles the shape of the action hero's mask.

3. Known as the "Mother Church of Country Music," Ryman Auditorium was originally a tabernacle for gospel meetings. A six-foot oak circle removed from the stage at the Ryman was embedded center stage at the Grand Ole Opry House when it was built in 1974.

4. Hot Chicken, one of Nashville's best-known culinary traditions, was created to inflict pain. When Thornton Prince's girlfriend suspected him of cavorting with other women in the 1930's, she added extra seasoning to the chicken batter. He liked the fiery flavor so much that he refined her recipe and opened a restaurant that became known as Prince's Hot Chicken Shack.

WASHINGTON D.C.

HOUSING SITE: MCKENDREE SIMMS-BROOKLAND UMC IS IN THE WOODRIDGE NEIGHBORHOOD

McKendree Simms-Brookland UMC was the combining of three historically black Methodist churches in the area: McKendree UMC, Sims UMC, and Brookland UMC. They provide a community lunch every Wednesday afternoon, and distribute food every Friday morning.

Washington, DC, is a unique city in that the primary purpose of its creation in 1790 was to serve as our nation's capital and house our federal government. Over the past 200 years, it has grown from a small city/county with plantations, small residential neighborhoods, and a few government buildings into a thriving city/state with its own culture, history, and economy. Its right to self-govern has shifted throughout the decades. It is a city under the control of Congress, but its citizens have had no voting Congressional representation since its inception. Washingtonians didn't receive the right to vote for President until 1965, and the current form of city government was authorized by Congress in 1970. Washington, DC, is the voteless capital of a democracy. The city symbolizes power and democracy to the world, but you can find the most powerless and disenfranchised inside it. A city whose residents still fight for their most basic rights as Americans.

Washington, DC, was also the first predominantly Black major city in the nation. However, in recent years, D.C. has undergone a significant change due to gentrification. It is one of the most gentrified cities in the US with over 40% of The District's neighborhoods experiencing change since 2000, making it consistently one of the most expensive cities to live in the United States. In these same areas, the black population has decreased by 23% while the white population has increased by over 200%. As neighborhoods have shifted due to gentrification, lower-income residents have been pushed out of their homes as more wealthy people move into the city. Over the span of 15 years, 20,000 Black Washingtonians have been displaced out of the city. Due to these changes, businesses and resources have focused development in the wealthier, white neighborhoods, leaving whole communities without equal access to daily necessities like grocery stores and healthy food options.

NEIGHBORHOODS

- There are around 131 unique neighborhoods inside the District of Columbia. Each is distinguished by its own history, culture, architecture, demographics, and geography.

FUN FACTS

1. It's the first predominantly Black populated city in the country.
2. The official music of DC is called Go-Go Music, a free-flowing funk made popular by Chuck Brown.
3. DC has its own special condiment sauce called Mambo Sauce, a red-orange sauce that is sweet and tangy that goes on all things fried.

Holy Disruptions

HOLY DISRUPTIONS is a way to embed rhythms of theological reflection into youth ministries so as to engage students and youth workers in robust theological dialogue born out of real-life experience that leads to reflective action in the world. Born out of the Center for Youth Ministry Training's Theology Together initiative, this framework for ministry has three movements: Interruption, Reflection, and Holy Disruption. Through this framework, we seek to position teenagers, alongside their youth ministers and leaders, as practical theologians and take seriously their ability to engage in robust theological dialogue born out of disruption and disorientation. Below are brief descriptions of the three movements:

INTERRUPTION (WOW)

Throughout the trip, we want youth to be on the lookout for moments in their day, as they serve and are with their group, that give them pause. Maybe someone said something, or they met someone who caught their attention. Maybe their experience that day challenged some of their assumptions about how the world works. Perhaps something made them think twice. We call that moment their "WOW" moment. It's from this moment that we begin our theological journey.

REFLECTION (WHY, WHAT)

We want them to explore "WHY that moment." Why did it stand out? What did it make them feel? Why did they feel that way? Then, we want them to explore "WHAT would our culture say about their moment?" What does a dinner conversation look like about this? How would the news report on that moment? How does it challenge the way they believe, think, or live? How is this different from what they experience back home?

HOLY DISRUPTION (GOD, ALIGN)

This is the movement where we engage how God views this moment and God's desires for us and those around us. What does God think about this? Scripture? Christian theology? How would Jesus respond? We choose at this moment to ALIGN or not with God's vision for this moment. How will they live differently (big or small) now that they have worked through this reflection? In light of all of this, how do they think God wants them to live differently?

LEADERSHIP TIPS

BASIC TIPS

◊ Know your space for your discussion groups and recognize its strengths and weaknesses
   - Size, set up, and atmosphere
   - Adjust where you need
◊ Be prepared, know your material before you gather
◊ Simple group rules for the week
   - Be here or be somewhere else
   - Love by listening
   - What's said here stays here
   - Be honest or be quiet
◊ Know and use the names of students
   - Communicates that they are known and valued

LEADING A REFLECTION

◊ Prior to having students share outloud have them write down their answers first
◊ Be willing to share your answers first. Say something like, "For instance, my WOW moment was ____."
◊ If the group is quiet don't be afraid to call students by name and ask them what their response is to the question.
◊ Be aware of who is speaking and who isn't.
   - Who talks a lot and who doesn't talk at all.
   - Work to try and create balance during your reflections and get multiple students to speak and participate.

PRAYER TOUR TIPS & TRICKS

◊ Set your students up for success while you drive by crafting a more reflective environment. Simple things can make a big difference:
   - Put low, calming music on in the background
   - Have everyone place their cell phones in a common space, covenanting together during this time to give their whole self to this experience
   - Be sure they have their journals out during the prayer tour
     - Turn to the pages that offer prompts, both prayer and art, to participate in during the prayer tour.
     - Have pens available just in case.

//ARRIVAL

THE THEME:

BLESSED

Bless, Blessing, Blessed

Have you ever wondered what a blessing actually is? We use that word so flippantly. We are #blessed, we "bless your heart" in the South, and we count our blessings. However, in most cases, blessing is about what we have and how we are blessed. We are blessed because we are privileged to fill in the blank. What fills that blank looks different to each of us, but what it has in common is that the ultimate subject of that blank is us and how we benefit from something or someone.

It's not wrong to recognize our blessings and be grateful for them. Practicing that gratitude is an incredibly important thing to do. Yet, we want to put that aside while you are on this trip. Blessed as a theme seeks to expand your definition of " blessing." To do that, we look to Jesus.

In Matthew 5:1-11, Jesus starts his most famous sermon, The Sermon on the Mount, by discussing who is " blessed " among the crowd. It may not surprise you, but it is those whom you would not think of: the poor in spirit, the mourners, the meek, the merciful, and the peacemakers, among others. It turns out it has nothing to do with possessions and a lot to do with our posture towards others and God.

We are blessed when we mourn for the overlooked and marginalized, for in our mourning, we act. We are blessed when our spirit aches for the suffering; out of a poor spirit, we move. We are blessed when we are pure in heart, for we begin to see God in all places. We are blessed when we make peace; when we make peace, we bring about God's kingdom on earth. May you be blessed on this trip by the blessing of others and God.

THEOLOGY TALK #1

WELCOME TO BLESSED AND HOLY DISRUPTIONS

SUMMARY

What does it mean to be Blessed?

You can imagine it's many things, especially positive things. Blessings are good. However, they also have a different meaning when you listen to how Jesus talks about being blessed. As we start exploring that together, we want you to be open to what God has to teach you about what it means to be blessed through your experiences and conversations at CSM.

Jesus's ideas about what it means to be blessed will initially appear topsy-turvy. They challenge you to rethink who is blessed, what it means to be blessed, why someone is blessed, and many other dimensions of blessings. As these collide with your experiences in the city, your understanding of blessings will be disrupted. That's a great thing! See these moments as instances where the Holy Spirit is breaking into your experience, nudging you to be open to the new things God has to teach you.

So, on this trip, CSM is asking you to serve in a likely unfamiliar city. You're being asked to risk your own comfort in order to have your life momentarily disrupted so that it will be permanently transformed.

Therefore, embrace the discomfort. Ask God to walk alongside you and your co-participants this week. Ask for an open heart and eyes to see what Being Blessed looks like in God's Kingdom.

What does it mean to be Blessed?

SCRIPTURE

[1] When Jesus[a] saw the crowds, he went up the mountain, and after he sat down, his disciples came to him. [2] And he began to speak and taught them, saying: [3] "Blessed are the poor in spirit, for theirs is the kingdom of heaven. [4] "Blessed are those who mourn, for they will be comforted. [5] "Blessed are the meek, for they will inherit the earth. [6] "Blessed are those who hunger and thirst for righteousness, for they will be filled. [7] "Blessed are the merciful, for they will receive mercy. [8] "Blessed are the pure in heart, for they will see God. [9] "Blessed are the peacemakers, for they will be called children of God. [10] "Blessed are those who are persecuted for the sake of righteousness, for theirs is the kingdom of heaven. [11] "Blessed are you when people revile you and persecute you and utter all kinds of evil against you falsely[b] on my account.

Scan to access
Theology Talk #1 video

THOUGHTS ON THE TALK

Journal, doodle, or take notes on the welcome Theology Talk here. What surprised you? Did you learn anything? Is there anything you want to investigate more? Jot it down here!

GROUP DISCUSSION QUESTIONS

1. To get us going, in what ways would you say you're blessed? Why?

2. What does the word "blessing" mean to you?

3. Now, think about this talk and share one thing that stands out to you the most. What stood out to you as you listened, especially regarding the idea of being blessed?

4. Read and summarize Matthew 5:1-11 together. What stands out to you? Why is this one of the first things Jesus preaches in his most famous sermon?

5. In light of our talk and scripture, what does it look like for you to be a blessing this week? What might it look like for those you encounter to be a blessing for you this week?

6. How might those two connect, you blessing others and others blessing you? Where do you think God is working in that, and how will you allow that to influence how you experience your time with CSM?

DAY ONE

DAILY CHALLENGE

What if you tried to see the city through God's eyes? Instead of "consuming" the city as a tourist today, open your eyes to the people you see and encounter. Ask the question, "How might God want me to interact with this person?"

DAILY DEVOTIONAL
Matthew 5:7-8

7 "Blessed are the merciful, for they will receive mercy.
8 "Blessed are the pure in heart, for they will see God.

City streets are filled with so much excitement and adventure. I don't know about you, but when I walk out onto them, it's always with a sense of anticipation. No matter what city you are in, there always seems to be something going on: buskers playing music for some change, eclectic outfits, bustling restaurants, and crowded streets filled with many different noises.

Cities are destinations. They are something to consume, enjoy, and be swept away by. However, experiencing a city solely like this risks missing a vital element of the city: its people.

For this reason, start your time in the city off through a different set of lenses. What if, instead of being entertained by the city, you sought to be merciful in the city? We are told, "Blessed are the merciful, for they will receive mercy." Maybe your blessing this trip is the fact that through your acts of mercy, you, yourself, experience the mercy of God. We are told, "Blessed are the pure in heart, for they will see God." Maybe your blessing this trip is opening your eyes to God's desires for the world: mercy, peace, and comfort. In seeing those desires, you begin to see how you can be agents of those things in the world around you, and when you do, you see God in the city. All of these cannot be done without the city's people, whom you are called to serve while you're here.

Welcome to the city streets. They are fun, eclectic, and full of life. They are also full of people in need of things like mercy, comfort, and especially love. May God, on this trip, grant you a pure heart and spirit of mercy so that you may have the blessing of being God's agents of grace, hope, peace, love, joy, and justice in the city!

PRAY

Prayer of St. Francis

Lord, make me an instrument of your peace:
where there is hatred, let me sow love;
where there is injury, pardon;
where there is doubt, faith;
where there is despair, hope;
where there is darkness, light;
where there is sadness, joy.
O divine Master, grant that I may not so much seek
to be consoled as to console,
to be understood as to understand,
to be loved as to love.
For it is in giving that we receive,
it is in pardoning that we are pardoned,
and it is in dying that we are born to eternal life.
Amen.

REFLECT

1. *What brought you here? Why did you come with us to CSM?*

2. *How do you hope to live differently here than you usually do at home?*

3. *How can you see the city you serve differently this week?*

RECEIVING HOSPITALITY

JENNA SCHMIDT

While you are here, we want to bring a new layer of intentionality to what you do. You might have noticed that one of the major rules we go over is being aware of yourself and your surroundings. We want you to be aware, just noticing a few things that it's easy not to see when we go on autopilot or when we don't care to look. Food is one of those things that's easy just to consume and not really think about.

This week, we will be learning about all the different reasons for thinking differently about what we consume. I want us to also think differently about the way we interact with the people whose restaurants we will be eating at. Throughout the gospels, the books of the Bible where we find the stories of Jesus, we see Jesus hanging out with people others didn't think he should be hanging out with and going over to tax collectors' houses and receiving food and hospitality from single or divorced women. Jesus regularly and happily received the hospitality of whoever was willing to offer it.

We are going to be eating at restaurants owned by families that have moved here for many different reasons. These families are offering us their food and culture as hospitality, and let's be intentional about receiving that. The way Jesus would. We would like to say that you are here this week to serve and learn with your time and your presence. Be fully present and aware of who is in front of you and how they might extend hospitality to you. Don't just mindlessly consume, but be intentional in partaking in the good news that ALL are welcome at Jesus' table.

DAILY DEBRIEF

This daily debrief can be done both individually and as a group. We encourage you to spend a little bit of time each night thinking about the day and reflecting on where you saw God at work and how that speaks to your experience as a Christian.

Start off with some basics about your day.
1. Where did you serve?
2. Where did you eat? What did you have?
3. Did you participate in any other activities?

INTERRUPTION: *We want you to start by exploring a moment that disrupted your day and made you think twice, to maybe say WOW.*

WOW!

Now, take a few moments to think of that moment of disruption, even if it was small.
- Did you meet someone, or did they say something that caught your attention?
- Was there a moment when things became more clear or when ideas and thoughts you had were suddenly challenged?
- Was there a time you had to think twice about how you think about yourself, the world, or God?

We call this your WOW moment. What made you say, "WOW!" today? Answer below:

REFLECTION: *This is a time to think about and navigate why that moment struck you and what our culture might say about it.*

WHY that moment?
Why did this moment stand out to you? What, if anything, surprised you? What emotions did your WOW moment make you feel? Why did you feel that way?

WHAT would our culture say about your moment?
What about your "WOW Moment" might challenge how you believe, think, or live? How is this different from what you've experienced back home?

HOLY DISRUPTION: *Finding where God intervenes in our experience and challenges us to respond in a way that aligns with God's desire for that moment.*

GOD What might God think about this?
What scripture(s) might shed light on your WOW moment? How would Jesus respond? What questions about faith did this moment create?

ALIGN How will you live differently?
In light of all of this, how do you think God wants you to live differently? How will this experience help you live differently? What does that look like tomorrow? Next week?

Use this page to continue your daily debrief notes.

DAY TWO

DAILY CHALLENGE

Encourage a teammate by telling them the gifts you see they are blessed with and how they can use their gifts to serve others.

DAILY DEVOTIONAL

1 Peter 4:7-11

7 The end of all things is near; therefore be serious and discipline yourselves for the sake of your prayers. 8 Above all, maintain constant love for one another, for love covers a multitude of sins. 9 Be hospitable to one another without complaining. 10 Like good stewards of the manifold grace of God, serve one another with whatever gift each of you has received. 11 Whoever speaks must do so as one speaking the very words of God; whoever serves must do so with the strength that God supplies, so that God may be glorified in all things through Jesus Christ. To him belong the glory and the power forever and ever. Amen.

TYLER - WASHINGTON, DC

If you have served with CSM DC in the past few years, you will likely have met Mr. Lou while serving at the Garden Guild. Mr. Lou ran the entire urban farm for almost ten years for FREE! That might sound crazy, but what is even crazier is that Mr. Lou didn't even know anything about gardening when he first started! His skills were all based on his 25 years of working in IT. But Mr. Lou soon realized that his skills in managing projects and people could be used creatively to run a farm that grows thousands of pounds of produce each year that can be given away for free to families in DC who need food. Like Mr. Lou, we are all BLESSED with unique skills and talents that have been gifted to us by God, and as the passage suggests, we are stewards of these gifts - meaning we are accountable for them. And the number one way we can use our gifts is by serving others.

We could look at this through Jesus' example of hiding a flame under a bushel. If we light a flame and put it under a bushel, then those around us cannot benefit from its light and cannot enjoy its warmth. But when the flame is free to shine, it gives light to those around us, who can see and be warmed by its heat. We can easily "hide" the blessings of our gifts and talents by using them for our gain, leaving others cold and in the dark. But Jesus tells us to "let our light shine before others, so that they may see our good works and give glory to our Father in heaven." - Our gifts are like the valuable resource of a flame, and we use those gifts to benefit and serve those around us. So, God does not Bless us for our own gain or self-indulgence but instead to love and serve others with "whatever gifts we have received."

While you are on this trip, I encourage you to find ways you can use your specific gifts in creative ways to love and serve those around you - whether it is a stranger you meet or your own teammates. And if you might not be certain what "gift(s)" God has blessed you with, take this week to allow God to reveal that to you. When we use the blessings God has given us to serve and love others, we "glorify God in all things through Jesus Christ."

PRAY

A Diary of Private Prayer (John Baillie)

O Heavenly Father, give me a heart like Jesus Christ, a heart more ready to serve than to be served, a heart moved by compassion towards those who are fragile and oppressed, a heart that longs to see the Kingdom of God established in our world. May it be Lord, that although my life is fulfilled and relatively untroubled, I would not be insensitive to the needs of those less fortunate than myself – make me sensitive to their needs and enable me to carry them in my heart. If I should have to face really difficult times, don't allow me to lick my wounds as if I were the only one in the world suffering; instead, let me give myself to the compassionate service of all who need my help. Let the power of my Lord Christ be powerful in me and may I be filled with His peace. Amen.

REFLECT

1. Why might we be called stewards of the "Grace" or 'Blessings" that God has given us? What does it mean to be accountable for your blessings?

2. What are the unique gifts that God has given you to serve your own community?

3. How can you use your gifts to love and serve the people in the city this week?

THOUGHTS ON THE TALK

Journal, doodle, or take notes on the first Theology Talk here. What surprised you? Did you learn anything? Is there anything you want to investigate more? Jot it down here!

GROUP DISCUSSION QUESTIONS

1. Think about this talk and share one thing that stands out to you the most. What amazed or shocked you as you listened?

2. What experiences on this trip have made you think about what it means to bless or be blessed?

3. How did the talk help you better understand your experiences on this trip so far?

4. Re-read and summarize Matthew 5:1-11 together again. What does that tell us about blessings in God's Kingdom? How does this challenge what you think about being blessed?

REFLECT

1. *What is the difference between sympathy and empathy and which do you think Jesus values more?*
2. *Has there been a time when someone acted like Jesus for you? If so, what did they do to help you get through the struggle?*
3. *What is one thing that you can do today to act like Jesus?*

DAILY DEBRIEF

This daily debrief can be done both individually and as a group. We encourage you to spend a little bit of time each night thinking about the day and reflecting on where you saw God at work and how that speaks to your experience as a Christian.

Start off with some basics about your day.
1. Where did you serve?
2. Where did you eat? What did you have?
3. Did you participate in any other activities?

INTERRUPTION: *We want you to start by exploring a moment that disrupted your day and made you think twice, to maybe say WOW.*

WOW!

Now, take a few moments to think of that moment of disruption, even if it was small.
- Did you meet someone, or did they say something that caught your attention?
- Was there a moment when things became more clear or when ideas and thoughts you had were suddenly challenged?
- Was there a time you had to think twice about how you think about yourself, the world, or God?

We call this your WOW moment. What made you say, "WOW!" today? Answer below:

REFLECTION: *This is a time to think about and navigate why that moment struck you and what our culture might say about it.*

WHY that moment?
Why did this moment stand out to you? What, if anything, surprised you? What emotions did your WOW moment make you feel? Why did you feel that way?

WHAT would our culture say about your moment?
What about your "WOW Moment" might challenge how you believe, think, or live? How is this different from what you've experienced back home?

HOLY DISRUPTION: *Finding where God intervenes in our experience and challenges us to respond in a way that aligns with God's desire for that moment.*

GOD What might God think about this?
What scripture(s) might shed light on your WOW moment? How would Jesus respond? What questions about faith did this moment create?

ALIGN How will you live differently?
In light of all of this, how do you think God wants you to live differently? How will this experience help you live differently? What does that look like tomorrow? Next week?

Use this page to continue your daily debrief notes.

DAY THREE

DAILY CHALLENGE

When you're out in the city today, see if you can find opportunities to praise God. It could be something minor, like smiling and complimenting someone or even taking a moment to thank God for the blessings he has given you in your own life.

DAILY DEVOTIONAL

PSALM 96:2-4

2 Sing to the Lord; bless his name;
tell of his salvation from day to day.
3 Declare his glory among the nations,
his marvelous works among all the peoples.
4 For great is the Lord and greatly to be praised;
he is to be revered above all gods.

Mission trips give us a chance to focus our attention on others and less on ourselves. You and your group may come in with the mindset of serving others well and blessing the community. Although the impact a mission trip can have for someone else is powerful, it's also great to come in with the mindset of blessing our God. How exactly do we bless God? Blessing God is different from God blessing us. God blesses us with strengths and gifts to do good works here on Earth. What God wants from us is our attention, our love, our praise. Blessing God is taking time to spread good news and sing of God's love and mercy on us.

This Psalm is helpful because it guides our hearts in ways to bless our Lord. We shall sing to the Lord and spread God's love to others. This is what God wants from us: to bring joy and song and praise. On Thursday nights at CSM, we have our worship night. This night is one of my favorites of our CSM activities because it brings us all together at the end of the week to sing and worship God and reflect on what God has shown us. While you are out in the community, you are a servant of God. Although it is wonderful to tell people about God's love and mercy, God wants us to put action to those words by going out and lending a helping hand to another person. This week, we can bless God by taking care of his people and his community.

PRAY

Mighty God, thank you for giving the gift of abundant, eternal life. The Bible says that whatever I do, whether in word or deed, I should do it all in the name of the Lord Jesus, giving thanks to God the Father. May my life be filled with thanksgiving and praise for your countless blessings. Give me assurance that you supply my every need through your generosity. May grace, mercy, and peace be with me, from God the Father and Jesus Christ the Son, in truth and love. It's in the name of Jesus Christ, our Lord, we pray. Amen.

REFLECT

1. *What are some ways that you can bless God during your CSM trip?*

2. *Who are some people in your life that you look up to that praise our Lord well?*

3. *When you go back home, how can you continue to bless God each day?*

THOUGHTS ON THE TALK

Journal, doodle, or take notes on the first Theology Talk here. What surprised you? Did you learn anything? Is there anything you want to investigate more? Jot it down here!

REFLECT

1. *Can you think of a time when someone went out of their way to serve you? How did you feel?*
2. *What are ways that we can practice this today as we are out in the city?*
3. *Where are places in your hometown that you think you could serve others?*

DAILY DEBRIEF

This daily debrief can be done both individually and as a group. We encourage you to spend a little bit of time each night thinking about the day and reflecting on where you saw God at work and how that speaks to your experience as a Christian.

Start off with some basics about your day.

1. Where did you serve?
2. Where did you eat? What did you have?
3. Did you participate in any other activities?

INTERRUPTION: *We want you to start by exploring a moment that disrupted your day and made you think twice, to maybe say WOW.*

WOW!

Now, take a few moments to think of that moment of disruption, even if it was small.

- Did you meet someone, or did they say something that caught your attention?
- Was there a moment when things became more clear or when ideas and thoughts you had were suddenly challenged?
- Was there a time you had to think twice about how you think about yourself, the world, or God?

We call this your WOW moment. What made you say, "WOW!" today? Answer below:

REFLECTION: *This is a time to think about and navigate why that moment struck you and what our culture might say about it.*

WHY that moment?
Why did this moment stand out to you? What, if anything, surprised you? What emotions did your WOW moment make you feel? Why did you feel that way?

WHAT would our culture say about your moment?
What about your "WOW Moment" might challenge how you believe, think, or live? How is this different from what you've experienced back home?

HOLY DISRUPTION: *Finding where God intervenes in our experience and challenges us to respond in a way that aligns with God's desire for that moment.*

GOD What might God think about this?
What scripture(s) might shed light on your WOW moment? How would Jesus respond? What questions about faith did this moment create?

ALIGN How will you live differently?
In light of all of this, how do you think God wants you to live differently? How will this experience help you live differently? What does that look like tomorrow? Next week?

Use this page to continue your daily debrief notes.

DAY FOUR

Be on the lookout for conversations where you can advocate for someone else. Try to add to that conversation in a meaningful way.

DAILY DEVOTIONAL

PROVERBS 31:8-9

8 Speak out for those who cannot speak,
for the rights of all the destitute.
9 Speak out; judge righteously;
defend the rights of the poor and needy.

AARON - KANSAS CITY, MO

In my friend group, we get into very unimportant arguments constantly. These include how we eat our cereal (crunchy or soggy), which cookie is best (oatmeal or chocolate chip), and whether a hotdog is a sandwich. These silly things constantly divide us. We pick sides, find our allies and enemies, and go to town roasting each other. Our arguments can go on for days or weeks, and we will throw digs at one another at any comically appropriate opportunity. These arguments can get loud and over the top quickly but are never serious. One friend, though, Hannah, is always the rational one. She can find some common ground between the two sides and always tries to find some form of resolution. Hannah is a peacemaker.

While my friend group's debates are lighthearted, there are many things in our world that are not and are vehemently fought over. Relationships sever, families split, and nations go to war over a multitude of issues that often overlap and affect us all. How are we to engage in these kinds of conflicts as people of faith?

The Scripture reading for today says to "speak for those who cannot speak" and to "defend the rights of the poor and needy." When those bigger and more important conflicts arise, we must learn to "judge righteously" and then advocate for those who need defending, those whose voices aren't being heard.

At its core, peacemaking involves empathy and compassion. We must recognize the humanity in all those involved and seek to address the root causes of conflict, not just address its surface manifestations. This often requires patience, humility, and a willingness to listen to differing perspectives. A peacemaker understands that sustainable peace is built on a foundation of justice, equity, and respect for all people.

PRAY

Litany of Peace (*Evangelical Lutheran Church in America*)
God, so many people are in pain. Teach us the way to peace. When people around us don't agree and think differently, Teach us to listen and try to understand. When we see people getting hurt, Teach us to speak up. When we see people treated poorly because of their skin color, or language, or religious belief, Teach us to be an example of love and acceptance. When we see war and conflict, Teach us how to make a difference and seek peace. When we see pain, Teach us to bring healing. When we feel confused and afraid, Remind us to talk to our friends, our family, and to you. In our lives, our neighborhoods, and the world, Teach us to pray and teach us the way of peace. Amen.

REFLECT

1. *What do you think it means to "judge righteously?"*
2. *In the Scripture reading, it says twice to "speak out" in defense of others. Are there certain topics or conversations where you don't feel comfortable speaking out? What about those topics makes you uncomfortable speaking out?*
3. *We are called to defend "the poor and needy." Those people include a vast multitude of people: those who are homeless and financially poor, migrants, minorities, those with disabilities, the incarcerated, the addicted, and many, many more. Are there any people groups that you feel you need to learn more about in order to be a good advocate? What are they?*

THOUGHTS ON THE TALK

Journal, doodle, or take notes on the first Theology Talk here. What surprised you? Did you learn anything? Is there anything you want to investigate more? Jot it down here!

REFLECT

1. *In what ways do our lives make it easy for us to ignore the cries of injustices happening around us? - or - What things in your life make it hard for you to hear/ distract you from hearing the cries of injustice by those around you?*

2. *Do we actively live our lives in service of the needs of others, or for our own comfort and happiness?*

3. *Does the way I live enhance or diminish the lives of other people?*

DAILY DEBRIEF

This daily debrief can be done both individually and as a group. We encourage you to spend a little bit of time each night thinking about the day and reflecting on where you saw God at work and how that speaks to your experience as a Christian.

Start off with some basics about your day.

1. Where did you serve?
2. Where did you eat? What did you have?
3. Did you participate in any other activities?

INTERRUPTION: *We want you to start by exploring a moment that disrupted your day and made you think twice, to maybe say WOW.*

WOW!

Now, take a few moments to think of that moment of disruption, even if it was small.

- Did you meet someone, or did they say something that caught your attention?
- Was there a moment when things became more clear or when ideas and thoughts you had were suddenly challenged?
- Was there a time you had to think twice about how you think about yourself, the world, or God?

We call this your WOW moment. What made you say, "WOW!" today? Answer below:

REFLECTION: *This is a time to think about and navigate why that moment struck you and what our culture might say about it.*

WHY that moment?
Why did this moment stand out to you? What, if anything, surprised you? What emotions did your WOW moment make you feel? Why did you feel that way?

WHAT would our culture say about your moment?
What about your "WOW Moment" might challenge how you believe, think, or live? How is this different from what you've experienced back home?

HOLY DISRUPTION: *Finding where God intervenes in our experience and challenges us to respond in a way that aligns with God's desire for that moment.*

GOD What might God think about this?
What scripture(s) might shed light on your WOW moment? How would Jesus respond? What questions about faith did this moment create?

ALIGN How will you live differently?
In light of all of this, how do you think God wants you to live differently? How will this experience help you live differently? What does that look like tomorrow? Next week?

Use this page to continue your daily debrief notes.

FINAL DAY

DAILY CHALLENGE

Our scripture this morning is Matthew 5:16. It talks about shining your
light for all the world to see. Think of some practical ways you want
your light to shine when you go home. Where in your community can you
serve? Who is on your mind after this trip that you can be a light to? As
you return home, ask God to begin revealing ways that you can continue
to live missionally so the work you're doing doesn't stop with this trip!

DAILY DEVOTIONAL

MATTHEW 5:16

16 In the same way, let your light shine before others,
so that they may see your good works
and give glory to your Father in heaven.

Through my work at CSM, I once heard a speaker talking about how she didn't consider herself a missionary, although she traveled the world to serve God and others. She considered this the lifestyle she was called to and lived "missionally." In her everyday life, she followed the call of God to be a light in the world. She did that whether it was internationally, on a trip in an urban city, in her own backyard, or even within her family.

A trip like this, serving in the city, lights a fire in all of us. Gaining these new experiences, meeting new people, setting ourselves aside, and serving others throughout our trip is the flame that is lit. As we wrap up this time and head home, it is up to you to keep the fire lit. In order to keep the flame burning, you have to stay connected with God. Prayer, studying scripture, surrounding yourself with a strong community, and continuing to serve others are all ways to do so.

As you go home and return to your everyday life, remember the people you met, the conversations you had, and the feeling you felt after a long day of service. Remember the stories you heard, the reality of life you saw that isn't like yours, and the gratefulness you feel after seeing the hardships of those in the city. Remember the light you carried throughout this experience as you gave food, planted seeds, or sorted clothes. That light remains as you go back to school, to work, and to your family and friends. That light is important in your own community!

The best part about a fire in Christ is how fast it can spread. For you all to leave here and continue to build the Kingdom of God, you must have a bright flame. Keep your flame alive so that in every conversation you have and every good deed you do, you are lighting a flame in others. You are spreading the Kingdom. In all you do, let it be to glorify God.

PRAY

Thank you, God, for all the life-changing experiences we have had on this trip. I pray that as we go home, we are able to take what we have learned and continue to serve. I pray that you continue to remind us that everyone is in need of your love and restoration. Help us find ways to serve those around us, knowing that it brings glory to You. We pray for safety as we return home. In Your name, we pray. Amen.

DISCUSS

Take a moment to think about how you felt before, during, and after each day of service.

1. *What expectations did you have coming into this trip?*
2. *What surprised you during your service work throughout the week?*
3. *How did you feel at the end of the day, knowing you had been able to show the love of Christ to those around you?*

WORSHIP, EDUCATIONAL ACTIVITY, PRAYER RESOURCES, AND REFLECTION

PRAYER PROMPTS FOR PRAYER TOUR

During the prayer tour, there will be multiple opportunities to pray out loud, or reflect silently. Sometimes it's hard to know what to say, reflect on or how to pray in that space. We have included some prayer prompts and Scripture below to help guide you for when you don't know what to pray or for during silent reflection:

Imagine holding the big, complicated thing in your hand and handing it to Jesus. In handing it to him, you can say:

- Come, Lord Jesus. Fix what is broken.
- This is _____ (scary, complicated, not the way it is supposed to be...). God, we need you to change it!

You can also use the words from these passages to pray for what you see around the city:

- **Psalm 36:5-9 NIV** - Your love, Lord, reaches to the heavens, your faithfulness to the skies. Your righteousness is like the highest mountains, your justice like the great deep. You, Lord, preserve both people and animals. How priceless is your unfailing love, O God! People take refuge in the shadow of your wings. They feast on the abundance of your house; you give them drink from your river of delights. For with you is the fountain of life; in your light we see light.

- **Psalm 67:1-3 NIV** - May God be gracious to us and bless us and make his face shine on us— so that your ways may be known on earth, your salvation among all nations. May the peoples praise you, God; may all the peoples praise you.

- **Isaiah 41:10 NIV** - So do not fear, for I am with you; do not be dismayed, for I am your God. I will strengthen you and help you; I will uphold you with my righteous right hand. *Continued on next page*

- ***Psalm 13 ESV*** - How long, O LORD? Will you forget me forever? How long will you hide your face from me? How long must I take counsel in my soul and have sorrow in my heart all the day? How long shall my enemy be exalted over me? Consider and answer me, O LORD my God; light up my eyes, lest I sleep the sleep of death, lest my enemy say, "I have prevailed over him," lest my foes rejoice because I am shaken. But I have trusted in your steadfast love; my heart shall rejoice in your salvation. I will sing to the LORD, because he has dealt bountifully with me.

- ***Psalm 79:9-11 ESV*** - Help us, O God of our salvation, for the glory of your name; deliver us, and atone for our sins, for your name's sake! Why should the nations say, "Where is their God?" Let the avenging of the outpoured blood of your servants be known among the nations before our eyes! Let the groans of the prisoners come before you; according to your great power, preserve those doomed to die!

- ***Psalm 79: 8-10 MSG*** - Hurry up and help us; we're at the end of our rope. You're famous for helping; God, give us a break. Your reputation is on the line. Pull us out of this mess, forgive us our sins — do what you're famous for doing!

ART PROMPTS FOR PRAYER TOUR

Throughout the tour or during moments of reflection, you may prefer to express your prayers / responses through art. We have included some prompts below to get you started:

- If you had a camera on the prayer tour, what would you take a picture of? Draw it here and write a caption as if you were posting it on social media.

- Illustrate where you saw God during the prayer tour, or what God is saying to you.

- Write a list of words or phrases that stick out to you during the prayer tour. Write them in the color that describes how you feel during the prayer tour.

- Circle the emotions that you feel during the prayer tour.

HAPPY JOYFUL SAD

ANGRY SURPRISED BORED

FRUSTRATED CONFUSED ANXIOUS

DISAPPOINTED CONFUSED OVERWHELMED OTHER (DRAW YOUR OWN)

REFLECTING ON WHAT YOU ARE SEEING

1. Think about what you saw during the prayer tour today. What was one thing you encountered during the tour that was meaningful or shocking to you? Something that made you say WOW? Something you don't want to forget?
2. Why was this encounter so meaningful or surprising to you?
3. Think about your culture - where you live, go to school or your family. What would your family or friends say about this WOW moment?
4. What do you think might be God's view of who and what is involved in this moment? How would God respond?
5. How might God want you to respond, live or act differently in response to this moment? How can you act as an agent and representative of God's Kingdom to bring change to what you saw today?

Spend some time reflecting on your Prayer Tour. This activity can be done in small groups or as one large group. Either way, use it to help unpack moments when you experienced something you didn't expect—your "WOW!" Moment.

INTERRUPTION
WOW!
- Start the discussion by asking someone in the group to share something from the prayer tour that made them say, "WOW." Take some time and allow people to respond.
- What was meaningful or shocking during the prayer tour? What grabbed your attention that you don't want to forget?

REFLECTION
WHY?
- What emotions rose up as you experienced the prayer tour?
- What exactly was your WOW moment from the prayer tour?
- Why was your WOW moment significant to you?

WHAT?
- What connections can you make between the prayer tour and the need for justice in the community?
- Think about where you come from - your family, friends, culture, values, etc. What might these things say or respond to the experiences from the prayer tour?
- How does your experience in your WOW moment compare and contrast to the normal expectations of the culture you come from?

HOLY DISRUPTION
GOD?
- What do you think might be God's view of the people and situations involved?
- What in the situation might make God: Angry? Smile? Sad or sorrowful?
- On what/whom might God have judgment or compassion in the story?
- What do you believe Christ would have done or said if he were in the story?
- How was God's love experienced (or not) by people in the story?
- What truth might God want to speak into the story?
- How was God at work in the story?

ALIGN!
- Where in your WOW moment is there an opportunity to offer yourself as an example of God's grace, love, compassion and mercy in the fight for justice in response to the prayer tour?
- How might God want you to live or act differently?
- How might we act as agents of God's Kingdom in the pursuit of social justice?
- What will you do with what you have learned today?

HOW DO YOU PRAY?

Several small details can be added or subtracted to enhance or specify one's prayer. These changes and gestures can be at your discretion.

OPEN VS. CLOSED HANDS
Open hands
- Open hands can be a gesture of giving. It is with open hands that we give gifts to those we care for, and it is with open hands that we give praise and thanks to God.
- Open hands can also show an openness to receive what God is offering. This can mean that one is open to receiving the grace and love that God offers but also that one is open to guidance and change. This gesture can say, "Here I am, God, I'm ready to receive what you're offering."

Closed fists
- Closed hands can represent strength and power. It shows that we are confidently holding on to God and God's promises.
- It can also be used to show that we are not yet ready to let go of something. This gesture can be used as a transition to an open-handed prayer.

OPEN VS. CLOSED EYES
Open eyes
- Keeping one's eye open during prayer can serve multiple purposes. It can be very practical in that if one moves during prayer, you can see where you're going and not disrupt others or your own prayer.
- It can also be a way of making your prayer more communal. When we see others around us in prayer or worship, we can join our prayer with theirs.

Closed eyes
- When one has their eyes open, it can bring distractions to mind that keep one from focusing on prayer. If this is the case, you might find it helpful to close your eyes.
- Despite most communal prayers being done with one's eyes closed, it is no more "spiritual" or "effective" than prayer with eyes open. It is merely done to help us focus and be intentional with our prayer.

SITTING VS. STANDING

Standing

- Standing is a posture of readiness. It shows that you are prepared to act and to move and God's calling and leading. If the purpose of prayer is to talk with God, we must be prepared to act when God does.

Sitting

- Sitting can be a posture of meditation. When God speaks, we sometimes need to sit metaphorically with it for a time to understand more fully what God is trying to convey to us. Sitting during prayer can be a physical gesture of sitting with God.
- Sitting is also a very practical posture. Some of us find it difficult to stand for long periods, so sitting is a perfectly acceptable posture for prayer. Our ability to commune with God is not hindered by our ability to perform a task.

RAISE ARMS ABOVE THE HEAD

- Raising one's hands is a very natural reaction to something great and exciting (Think of any sporting event and your team scores). This posture can be a great way to express the joy you're experiencing in prayer.
- This gesture is also associated with gratitude and with power. We raise our hands knowing that God is in control and we are responding with thanksgiving.

KNEELING

- Kneeling is a traditional posture of humility. When we kneel, we recognize that there is someone who is deserving of our respect and honor. In kneeling prayer, we humble ourselves before God and recognize God's greatness.
- Because of this, kneeling is a great posture for prayers of confession. We can bring our failings and shortcomings to God, knowing we will receive God's grace and mercy. Then, we can rise from our kneeling posture with confidence in that grace.

PROSTRATION

- Prostration has a long history in Christian worship and prayer. Dating back to worship in the Old Testament of Scripture, the people of God have used this posture to represent complete vulnerability. This position takes the most work to get into and to get out of. If some threat comes at us during this posture, it would be very difficult to respond to. Therefore, while prostrating, we wholly and completely trust in God's protection.
- It is in this position that we can recognize our own frailty and that we can not do everything. This is a posture of true humility.

LAYING FLAT ON BACK WITH ARMS AND LEGS SPREAD

- This is a posture of rest. When we sleep at night, it is often in this position. Here we can rest with God in prayer. We can trust that when we rise, we will be energized and prepared to do the work that calls us to.

LOTUS POSITION

- This position creates an opportunity for reflection and contemplation. It is in this posture that we sit with God and ponder how God is trying to speak. We can ground ourselves to the present moment and our environment to see how God is moving and working. We leave our arms uncrossed to represent our openness to God's leading.

MEANDERING

- For some of us, sitting or lying still can be difficult. Slow meandering or walking is a great alternative. Being mindful of those around us, we can aimlessly wander around this space in prayer. This type of prayer is not focused on walking but rather to help us focus on moving in step with God. We are all on a journey, and God wants us to be aware of God's presence on that journey. Take your time and enjoy the journey.

URBAN PLUNGE
RESOURCES

Use this page to jot down any notes or thoughts you might have during your urban plunge.

Use this page to jot down any notes or thoughts you might have during your urban plunge.

Spend some time reflecting on your Prayer Tour. This activity can be done in small groups or as one large group. Either way, use it to help unpack moments when you experienced something you didn't expect—your "WOW!" Moment.

INTERRUPTION
WOW!
- Start the discussion by asking someone in the group to share something from the prayer tour that made them say, "WOW." Take some time and allow people to respond.
- What was meaningful or shocking during the prayer tour? What grabbed your attention that you don't want to forget?

REFLECTION
WHY?
- What emotions rose up as you experienced the prayer tour?
- What exactly was your WOW moment from the prayer tour?
- Why was your WOW moment significant to you?

WHAT?
- What connections can you make between the prayer tour and the need for justice in the community?
- Think about where you come from - your family, friends, culture, values, etc. What might these things say or respond to the experiences from the prayer tour?
- How does your experience in your WOW moment compare and contrast to the normal expectations of the culture you come from?

HOLY DISRUPTION
GOD?
- What do you think might be God's view of the people and situations involved?
- What in the situation might make God: Angry? Smile? Sad or sorrowful?
- On what/whom might God have judgment or compassion in the story?
- What do you believe Christ would have done or said if he were in the story?
- How was God's love experienced (or not) by people in the story?
- What truth might God want to speak into the story?
- How was God at work in the story?

ALIGN!
- Where in your WOW moment is there an opportunity to offer yourself as an example of God's grace, love, compassion and mercy in the fight for justice in response to the prayer tour?
- How might God want you to live or act differently?
- How might we act as agents of God's Kingdom in the pursuit of social justice?
- What will you do with what you have learned today?

READING THEOLOGY WITH FRIENDS RESOURCES

We want to invite you on a journey.

A journey in reading something difficult and coming to understand it together—It is a journey of reading something difficult and coming to understand it together—with the friends gathered around you right now. That might sound a little strange. But in fact, reading wasn't really meant to happen alone. Whether the New Testament letters of Paul or the Greek poetry of Homer, in ancient times, reading was meant to be a communal activity.

Today, we're reading theology, which means the study or talk about God. The authors are theologians, and their work is an attempt to put forth a reasoned explanation of some aspect of God through the reading of scripture, exploring traditional Christian beliefs, and considering people's experiences with God.

This isn't easy, especially since God is...well, God.

And that's why we're going to do this together.

YOUR ROLE ON THE JOURNEY

We're going to ask you to read, think, and discuss a theological text with other people.

But hear this:

You don't have to know the Bible well.
You don't need to have all your theology figured out.
All you need to do is read, think, and discuss.
To wonder aloud and ask questions.
To point out things that don't make sense and the ones that spark something inside you.

And maybe (just maybe) this process will help you discover a bolder, more real, and vivid understanding of the Mysterious God who calls us to be God's own people.

Are you ready?

Great. Let's begin. . . together.
For this journey, we recommend that someone read the texts aloud (change readers every paragraph or so) while the rest of the group follows along. It's easier to remember and understand something you're both hearing and seeing..
After each section, we'll pause to allow everyone to respond to questions in writing. Then, we'll discuss what we each wrote together before moving to the next section. Reading Theology With Friends

MISSIONAL: JOINING GOD IN THE NEIGHBORHOOD

SPEAK THE PEACE: SHALOM - ALAN J. ROXBURGH

On the other hand, in Luke's Gospel, shalom[1] functions as a lot more than just a greeting. In the way Luke is writing his Gospel, we will note that when these disciples of Jesus enter into the towns and villages, they are among people who know the old stories but have lost any sense of their vitality. They are getting by and making do with life, keeping their heads low to avoid trouble from the Romans and the authorities. When they hear the language of shalom on the lips of these strangers who are followers of Jesus, it reminds them of God's promised future. Shalom is the promise of Jubilee[2] and the rule of God among them. They must have heard this word as a shock because it would be suggesting that the exile is over.

In the postresurrection narratives of John's Gospel, the story is told of the disciples (not just the Twelve but a much larger group of men and women) gathered in an upstairs room with the door bolted for fear the authorities would come to kill them as they had Jesus (20:19-23). These were terrified people for whom the story of Jesus had gone terribly wrong. All bets were off; nothing had turned out as expected. Confusion and disorientation filled their hearts.

Then Jesus steps into the room, and the text makes it clear he did not come in through the door. To assuage their shock and terror, he shows them the wounds in his hands and sides - signs that he was not an apparition but, in fact, the resurrected Lord. John is focused on emphasizing the utter materiality and physicality of this moment. The disciples, in John's story, are not projecting their desires or playing at wishful thinking to compensate for the utter loss of hope. This was Jesus standing before them in his resurrected body. The next points in John's account are crucial.

---

[1] A common Hebrew greeting meaning peace.

[2] The 50 year cycle in which, according to the book of Leviticus, indentured servants would be released, debts would be forgiven, and property returned to the original owners.

[3] To make less intense.

STOP! Choose one box below and take three minutes to complete the statement. Be ready to share!

CONFUSED THESE concepts, ideas, or points the author has made don't make sense to me... 　**ASK:** *Who can shed some light on this?*	**MY EXPERIENCE** The author helps me see my own experience of people, the world, God or myself in this new way... 　**ASK:** *Who else has had this experience?*
MY BELIEFS I'd never before thought about THIS idea that the author presents...(Do you believe the author is correct? Why?) 　**ASK:** *Who else doesn't believe it? Who does?*	**GRASP IT** Another WAY to explain one of the author's main points is this... 　**ASK:** *Do others think that's the point?*

John is a theologian. Like Luke, he is writing a theohistorical[4] account of Jesus and the birth of the church. John weighs his words carefully to construct the point of his story. Those gathered in that upper room had pinned their hopes on Jesus's being the fulfillment of God's promises in the Scriptures. Jesus was to be the one who brought the good news that God's promises were being fulfilled - this is what was involved in the times being filled up and coming to completion.

When, therefore, Jesus stands in that room and says to those gathered, "Shalom," he is not speaking in what might appear to our psychologically driven, modern Western ear as an effort to quell the fear of those in the room. In this word Jesus was picking up the expectations of Israel for the shalom (kingdom, reign, rule, future) of God. In this word Jesus was announcing that the promises of God's coming reign are now being fulfilled in his resurrected presence.

This is the same meaning of the word shalom Luke is using in 10:5-6. When the seventy go to the towns and villages, they are announcing that God's future has come in Jesus. The seventy announce good news, but what is the nature of this good news? One suspects that for at least some in those towns and villages, it must have been a terrifying announcement they did not want to hear in the midst of empire occupation. The healing of the sick was, itself, a sign that in these followers of Jesus the promised kingdom of God was coming. Exile was over!

STOP

Let's see if we can narrow down Roxburgh's argument a bit.
- What would you say is Roxburgh's main point?
- How does the practice of "speaking" peace relate to blessing?
- How could "Shalom" be a blessing for the world today? What might that look like?
- What questions do you still have?
- What's our big takeaway from this reading?

---

4 Theological history.

LIFE OF THE BELOVED

HENRI J. M. NOUWEN

I am increasingly aware of how much we fearful, anxious, insecure human beings are in need of a blessing. Children need to be blessed by their parents and parents by their children. We all need each other's blessings - masters and disciples, rabbis and students, bishops and priests, doctors and patients.

Let me first tell you what I mean by the word "blessing." In Latin, to bless is benedicre. The word "benediction" that is used in many churches means literally: speaking (dictio) well (bene) or saying good things of someone. That speaks to me. I need to hear good things said of me, and I know how much you have the same need. Nowadays, we often say: "We have to affirm each other." Without affirmation, it is hard to live well. To give someone a blessing is the most significant affirmation we can offer. It is more than a word of praise or appreciation; it is more than pointing out someone's talents or good deeds; it is more than putting someone in the light. To give a blessing is to affirm, to say "yes" to a person's Belovedness. And more than that: To give a blessing creates the reality of which it speaks. There is a lot of mutual admiration in this world, just as there is a lot of mutual condemnation. A blessing goes beyond the distinction between admiration or condemnation, between virtues or vices, between good deeds or evil deeds. A blessing touches the original goodness of the other and calls forth his or her Belovedness.

STOP! Choose one box below and take three minutes to complete the statement. Be ready to share!

CONFUSED
THESE concepts, ideas, or points the author has made don't make sense to me...
 	
    ASK: Who can shed some light on this?
	MY EXPERIENCE
	The author helps me see my own experience of people, the world, God or myself in this new way...
	
	    ASK: Who else has had this experience?

MY BELIEFS
I'd never before thought about THIS idea that the author presents...(Do you believe the author is correct? Why?)
 	
    ASK: Who else doesn't believe it? Who does?
	GRASP IT
	Another WAY to explain one of the author's main points is this...
	
	    ASK: Do others think that's the point?

...I recognized the importance of blessing and being blessed and reclaimed it as a true sign of the Beloved. The blessings that we give to each other are expressions of the blessing that rests on us from all eternity. It is the deepest affirmation of our true self. It is not enough to be chosen. We also need an ongoing blessing that allows us to hear in an ever-new way that we belong to a loving God who will never leave us alone, but will remind us always that we are guided by love on every step of our lives. Abraham and Sarah, Issac and Rebecca, Jacob, Leach, and Rachel, they all heard that blessing and so became the fathers and mothers of our faith. They lived their long and often painful journeys without ever forgetting that they were the blessed ones. Jesus, too, heard that blessing after John the Baptist had baptized him in the Jordan. A voice came from heaven saying: "You are my Beloved Son, on you my favor rests." This was a blessing, and it was that blessing that sustained Jesus through all the praise and blame, admiration and condemnation that followed. Like Abraham and Sarah, Jesus never lost the intimate knowledge that he was the "blessed one."

STOP

Let's see if we can narrow down Nouwen's argument a bit.
- What is Nouwen's main point?
- What would it look like for someone to genuinely "bless" you?
- If a blessing is the "deepest affirmation of our true self," what does that look like in practice with others?
- What questions do you still have?
- What's our big takeaway from this reading?

EVANGELISM AND DISCIPLESHIP

THE GOD WHO CALLS, THE GOD WHO SENDS - WALTER BRUEGGEMAN

The God who calls is the God who sends. This God sends because God has compelling authority to issue imperatives that anticipate ready acceptance, and God has a compelling passion for what is to be effected and enacted in the world that this God governs.

The sending of Abraham (and Sarah) is perhaps the overarching missional dispatch in all of Scripture. God issues to Abraham an initial imperative. "Go." Then God makes extravagant promises to Abraham concerning land, name, and blessing. But the sending culminates with this responsibility entrusted to Abraham: "By you all the families of the earth shall be blessed" (Gen. 12:3)

Israel exists to cause a blessing that is to be widely shared. "Blessing" is not a religious or moral phenomenon[5] in the world of Israel, but is a characteristic feature of creation that is fruitful and productive. Blessing means that the world should be generous, abundant, and fruitful, effecting generative fertility, material abundance, and this-worldly prosperity - shalom in broadest scope. Israel's life is to make the world work better according to the intention of the Creator.

---

[5] A fact or situation that is observed to exist or happen, especially one whose cause or explanation is in question.

STOP! Choose one box below and take three minutes to complete the statement. Be ready to share!

CONFUSED
THESE concepts, ideas, or points the author has made don't make sense to me...
    ASK: *Who can shed some light on this?*
	MY EXPERIENCE
	The author helps me see my own experience of people, the world, God or myself in this new way...
	    ASK: *Who else has had this experience?*

MY BELIEFS
I'd never before thought about THIS idea that the author presents...(Do you believe the author is correct? Why?)
    ASK*: Who else doesn't believe it? Who does?*
	GRASP IT
	Another WAY to explain one of the author's main points is this...
	    ASK: *Do others think that's the point?*

Leaders: Take time for sharing & then discussion using the 'ASK' questions before continuing.

Genesis 12:1-3 functions, on the one hand, as a hinge to what follows. 2 The passage looks forward toward the entire family of Abraham that exists in order to evoke blessing in the world. More stunning, on the other hand, is the awareness that this mandate looks back to Genesis 3-11, that is, to all the nations of the world that are under curse: Adam and Eve, Cain and Abel, the Flood, and the tower. All of these narratives tell of the families of the earth becoming alienated from God and living in contradiction to the will of God. In God's missional mandate to Abraham, Abraham is called to exist so that the general condition of curse in the world is turned to a general condition of blessing, life, and well being. Israel's mission is to mend the world in all its parts.

Paul quotes this very text from Genesis in urging that the gospel pertains to the Gentiles: "And the scripture, foreseeing that God would justify the Gentiles by faith, declared the gospel beforehand to Abraham, saying, 'All the Gentiles shall be blessed in you'" (Gal. 3:8). The wondrous phrase of Paul, "gospel beforehand," is a recognition that from the outset the good intention of the Creator God cannot be limited to any ethnic or racial or national enclave. Here is the warrant for a vision of a community of shalom, rooted in God's own vision of the creation, that repudiates every death-bringing distinction and every leverage of some over against others. Moreover, the mandate in Genesis is not to make the nations over into Israelites, nor even to make them Yahwists[1]. The focus is kept upon the improvement of the quality of life as willed by the creator God.

STOP

Let's see if we can narrow down Brueggeman's argument a bit.
- What is Brueggeman's main point?
- He talks about "blessing" as something we are sent to do. What would that look like out in the world today?
- In light of this understanding of blessing, what would Brueggeman say isn't a blessing?
- What questions do you still have?
- What's our big takeaway from this reading?

---

[1] Those who worship Yahweh, the Hebrew word for God.

NOTES, DOODLES, ETC

NOTES, DOODLES, ETC

NOTES, DOODLES, ETC

CITY SERVICE MISSION

Founded in 1988 as "Center for Student Missions," CSM sought to bridge the gap between the suburbs and the urban centers in the United States with a mission to provide effective short-term Christian mission experiences for youth and adults in urban settings.

Today, we proudly call ourselves "City Service Mission" and continue to provide urban ministry experiences for junior high, senior high, college, adult, and family groups.

We offer serving opportunities in 4 cities from the east coast to the west coast of the United States. In each city, we partner with dozens of faith-based and nonfaith-based organizations that are already seeking to meet a specific need in their community. We recognize that God has called us into this ministry, and that by coming alongside these existing organizations, we are helping provide a solution for the city.

To learn more about CSM check out www.csm.org

CYMT

A Brief intro to CYMT: The Center for Youth Ministry Training (CYMT) is a non-profit organization based in Nashville, Tennessee that, through a graduate residency program and other initiatives, equips youth ministers and communities of faith to develop innovative, effective, and theologically informed ministries so youth may experience the love and grace of Jesus Christ. CYMT connects with aspiring youth leaders and ministries across the country.

To learn more about CYMT check us out at our website www.cymt.org

On our website we have more resources we would love to share with you!

THEOLOGY TOGETHER

Brief Intro to Theology Together: Theology Together is a different way to experience and do youth ministry. It seeks to educate youth workers in tandem with the teenagers with whom they minister while changing the climate of congregational youth ministry as together they introduce theological dialogue, vocational discernment, and reflective action into the fabric and flow of youth ministry in the local church. By creating an environment in which youth are engaged in theological discussion and reflective action with their youth leaders, not only are youth expanded in their theological knowledge and conceptions, but youth leaders are simultaneously trained in the art of engaging young people in theological dialogue. An added benefit is that youth and adults are prepared to return to the congregational context together to further expand the theological repertoire and engagement of the entire youth ministry.

Rather than focusing on discrete youth drawn from congregational ministries, Theology Together seeks to form a cohort of youth and adults who experience robust theological thought and dialogue together. A primary focus is to equip these youth and youth pastors together to change the climate of youth ministry in their congregations by giving them the tools to initiate theologically robust practices of youth ministry in their congregational contexts. Theology Together initiatives serve to instigate, energize, and support ongoing transformational practices in the congregation rather than being the primary site of transformation for youth.

To learn more about Theology Together check us out at our website www.cymt.org/theology-together

On our website we have more resources we would love to share with you! Well, you can. Holy Disruptions, the reflection methodology used for your reflection times in this journal is being developed into a youth ministry curriculum that you can use each week in your church! We would love for you to check it out.

Scan the QR code for our
Holy Disruptions Curriculum.

Made in the USA
Columbia, SC
25 May 2024

36005051R10039